my journey...
from skepticism to faith

josh mcdowell
with cristóbal krusen

Tyndale House Publishers, Inc.
Carol Stream, Illinois

Visit Tyndale online at www.tyndale.com.

TYNDALE and Tyndale's quill logo are registered trademarks of Tyndale House Publishers, Inc.

My Journey . . . from Skepticism to Faith

Designed by Erik M. Peterson

Edited by Bonne Steffen

ISBN 978-1-4143-3437-0

Printed in the United States of America

17 16 15 14 13 12
7   6   5   4   3   2

1

I woke up earlier than usual that day. It was still dark outside. I dressed quickly to do my chores, distracted by the suspense that had been building for days. Leaving the house, I walked to the barn as I had done a thousand times before.

Perhaps today will be the day, I thought, feeding a bucket of oats to my horse, Dolly. She looked at me with her big brown eyes that always set me at ease. I could almost hear her thinking, *Can I come with you?*

I laughed and stroked her muzzle. "We'll see, Dolly. We'll see." She neighed softly, comfortingly. I hurried to do my other chores, but even though I was still unfinished at seven o'clock, I ran into the house looking for Mom. *The chores can wait,* I thought to myself.

In the kitchen, Wayne Bailey, our hired hand, was washing dishes. He was a tall, thin man with a long, pointed nose. Sometimes I thought he looked scary; other times I thought he looked comical as he walked about the house with his apron on, stooping to sweep up the dust in the corners or from under our worn furniture.

"Where's Mom?"

Wayne looked up from his dishes, his eyes narrowing. "Why do you wanna know?" he asked.

I played dumb, pretending to yawn. "Just wonderin'."

"She's out with your dad."

My eyes widened. "They movin' the house already?" I was so excited that I could scarcely get the words out.

"What do you need to know for?"

I studied Wayne's face for a clue. "They're movin' the house, ain't they!" I exclaimed.

Wayne pretended to scrub extra hard on a frying pan. His silence said it all. I ran to my room to change into clean bib overalls and a red checkered shirt I'd set aside for the occasion. Reappearing moments later, I tucked my shirt into my pants and headed for the door.

Wayne glared at me. "Your mom said you can't go nowhere 'til you finish your chores!"

"The chores is finished!" I retorted, bolting out the door.

In the distance, I could see people walking back and forth along the ridge of a nearby hill. There were cars and trucks parked along the sides of the hill as well. I ran as fast as my eleven-year-old legs could carry me. This was one event I was not going to miss. No, sir. This was like having the circus come to town—only better. The circus was coming into my own backyard!

My older brother, Wilmot Jr., or "Junior" as we called him, was going to move the itinerant farmworkers' house, situated on the top of the hill, to about a mile or so down the road. For some reason, this made my parents terribly upset. Every time the subject came up for discussion, Mom would cry. I wasn't sure why this upset her and my dad; they wouldn't tell me, though there was talk about how Junior's wife was dominating him, or some such thing, and putting foolish ideas in his head.

There was also talk of a "law suit" and how Junior was taking Mom and Dad to the "cleaners." I asked Mom what a "law suit" looked like and why it cost so much to get it cleaned. The questions only made her more upset.

"You're too young to understand," she'd say, going on to give me an explanation anyway. It seemed that Junior claimed my dad had promised him the house. My dad claimed he had done no such thing, but who knows? Dad was a heavy drinker, and he'd say things he later regretted or didn't remember having said. His daily drinking regimen was between two and three bottles of cheap wine. Sometimes he'd get violent (usually as he was getting drunk), then he'd be incoherent and passive.

For me, however, all this talk about "lies" and "law suits" was best left to the grown-ups to sort out. My mind was caught up in other things. *How are they going to move a house?* I wondered. That was the question I wanted answered. Were helicopters going to fly in, lift the house up, and carry it across the mile or so of farmland to its new location? Or maybe airplanes were going to swoop down and haul it away on thick, strong ropes. I had no idea, but I sure wasn't going to miss the show.

I was out of breath by the time I reached the top of the hill. Already, big tractors were positioned around the house, and a crew of workmen was securing the sides of the house with lines. I saw my mom and dad glaring at Junior, who was standing next to the house. A crowd of neighbors and folks from town were laughing and carrying on while they dug up the shrubbery and small trees my mom had planted around the house. I'd been expecting a party, but this had an odd feel to it. Something wasn't right.

I'd been expecting a party, but this had an odd feel to it. Something wasn't right.

I watched as my father walked over and grabbed Junior by the wrist to stop him from digging up the plants. Junior jerked his arm away, and Dad stumbled backward. Mom made her way toward the crowd as well, waving her handkerchief as if calling for a truce. The crowd ignored her, gathering around Dad and scolding him like an ignorant child. I heard words that turned my ears red. Then the crowd turned on Mom and began insulting her, using the filthiest, most vile language you can imagine. For a moment I looked into the faces of these "good folks" I had known all my life. How could they be calling my mom and dad such names? Weren't they our friends?

My dad, who had already been drinking that

morning, slipped on the muddy ground and fell on his backside, drawing further jeers from the crowd. I ran to my mother, afraid she might fall, too, as she tried to help him up. I'll never forget the look on her face. She looked at me with the eyes of someone drowning, someone who had struggled to stay afloat amid swirling currents and was now too weak to continue. I could see her giving up and letting go, resigning herself to a watery grave. I looked down at my freshly pressed bib overalls and red checkered shirt. There were flecks of mud on my pants. It had started to rain.

I looked around once more. This wasn't going to be a party, I realized. There weren't going to be airplanes moving a house down the road either. My disappointment was overshadowed by the harsh lessons burned into my heart like a branding iron. I had never known love in my home, but now I saw with my own eyes that it seemed like our neighbors had no love for us either. There was no love anywhere in the world. And I remember thinking, *There is no hope. There is no love and there is no hope.* And then my mind went blank.

───────

The next thing I knew I was running down the other side of the hill toward the barn, crying and screaming in front of everyone. At one end of the barn were stalls containing wheat, oats, and shelled corn for mixing cattle feed. I ran up the steps to the grain bins, passed through a large door, and lowered the door's heavy iron latch behind me. There were two windows with louvered blinds in the room. I knocked out the sticks holding up the blinds and, there in the darkness, crawled into the shelled-corn bin and buried myself up to my neck in the corn.

I wanted to die. Not because the "party" on the hill had gone sour; not because my parents were humiliated by false friends or my brother hated his own family; but because all of these things—and more— had combined to make me bitter. I felt such shame.

I cursed God between the sobs erupting from inside me. God—if he even existed—had abandoned me. And if he did exist, if he had stood in front of me right at that moment, I would have attacked him with every ounce of strength in my body. I hated him more than anything else in the world. Well, more than almost anything.

My father was right up there too. I cursed and damned him over and over, as if taking an oath. The town drunk. The coward who'd beat my mother every time he had too much to drink. Even now, he was probably out looking for one of his wine bottles, which he kept hidden around the farm. He was no father. He was a miserable drunk who had children so he could have workers on the farm. He'd get what he had coming to him. I'd see to that.

An hour passed, then two, then three. I began to get hungry. It became clear no one was going to come and look for me. I was alone, abandoned. It seemed no one cared whether I lived or died.

Eventually I struggled out of the corn bin and made my way to the door with the heavy latch. I pushed open the door, blinded by the glare of the bright sunlight. I squinted, wondering if, perhaps, I'd see someone there. Someone who had come to look for me. My mother, perhaps.

She'd be calling my name, wanting to comfort me. But no one was there. Just the sound of blowing wind.

I remember thinking, *There is no love in the world. No purpose. No God.*

I shut the door to the grain stalls and walked down the steps to the main floor of the barn. *We live like the animals*, I remember thinking. *And one day, I'll die like an animal. We all will. There is no love in the world. No purpose. No God.* My eyes began to adjust to the bright light just as my heart began to adjust to the new realities of my existence. The innocence of childhood evaporated like morning mist.

2

My one solace was my horse, Dolly. I loved to sit with her early in the morning, watching her eat oats, and talking with her about anything and everything. She always listened and never talked back. I was with her the next morning when I heard the cows mooing loudly and my father cursing.

"Let's see," I said to Dolly. "My guess is he's tryin' to connect a milk hose to the air pump but can't get it on. What do you think?"

Dolly looked back at me with her warm brown eyes and munched contentedly on her oats. "Good thing he can't milk you," I said. "He'd probably make a mess of that, too." Just then I heard another voice, a voice that sent chills up my spine and caused my body to tense. Mother. She was shouting at my father. For a moment, even the cows grew silent as my mother scolded my father at the top of her lungs. "You'll kill these cows if you leave them connected to the milking machines like this!" The cows began to moo again, but not before I heard a lone piercing shriek.

I got to my feet and ran toward the other end of the

barn. My mother's screams were louder now, as were the grunts and curses of my father. I turned the corner to see the sickening, all-too-familiar sight. My drunken father was beating my mother with a rubber milk hose, striking her repeatedly with all his force. Before I could reach them, he knocked her to the ground, where she fell in a trench next to the cows and rolled about helplessly in the manure.

I was on my father in an instant, pummeling him and kicking and spitting and cursing him all at once. Fortunately, Dad was not a big man. And thankfully, when I intervened in the altercations he would have with my mother, he never turned on me. Somehow, somewhere in his darkened mind, I suppose I caused a shock wave to go off, a reality check that made him break off his abuse and stagger from the barn. But I wasn't done with him yet. I followed Dad as he walked out, yelling at him at the top of my voice.

"I'll kill you one day! You hear me? I'll kill you!" I threw a hammer at him but missed. "I'll kill you in your sleep! I'll put a kitchen knife in you, stick it right in your heart and twist it side to side!" Dad never turned around.

And then I heard my mother's voice crying for help. She couldn't get up. I couldn't lift her up either. She was way too heavy for me (Mom was short and weighed well over three hundred pounds). I knelt beside her, wiping the blood from her face and crying with her. She looked at me with the same look I had seen on the hill the day before, the eyes of the drowning woman about to let go and disappear under the water. "He don't mean it," she said to me softly. "He don't mean it."

Shut up! I screamed inside. *He does mean it.* And so did I. Oh, how I hated him. I wanted to do to him what he had done to her. I wanted him to feel the pain he had caused others. I wanted Dad dead so bad I could taste it.

"Get Wayne," said my mother hoarsely.

Wayne knew the routine, because it happened on a regular basis. Between the two of us, we'd get Mom on her feet again and back in the house, where she'd lie in bed for several days, recovering. Her injuries weren't always due to my dad's abuse. Because of her excessive weight she often fell doing chores around the house, invariably throwing her hips out of joint.

"Wayne!" I shouted as I ran into the house. Wayne was in his room. I ran upstairs and poked my head in the door. His room was always neat and tidy, made homey with his collection of teacups—of all things. In addition, Wayne had parakeets in a cage: colorful, chirpy little creatures that contrasted with our drab farm surroundings.

He already knew what had happened from all the shouting. He looked at me with that familiar smirk, walked over beside me, and knelt down to look me directly in the eyes. I recoiled slightly. He always had bad breath. Yet there was a certain tenderness in his eyes too, a certain understanding. He put his hand on my shoulder, and when I pulled back he looked hurt. I ignored it.

"Mom needs help," I said. Wayne's hands moved toward my face, this time wiping the tears from my cheeks. He spoke in a reassuring voice. "No use frettin' about it, Josh. Let's go see what we can do."

Wayne and I walked downstairs and out the front door of the house. This time I let him keep his hand on my shoulder. Mom was where we had left her, but she had more manure on her now. We helped her to her feet, and a few hours later, she was cleaned up and in her bed, resting. As for me, I was late for school.

3

It's hard to believe, but sometimes Mom and Dad would get along and do things together, like driving from Michigan to California to visit relatives. I always had to stay home with Wayne. Mom's instructions were explicit: "Do everything Wayne tells you to do. If you're disobedient, I'll give you a good thrashing when I get home."

"Why don't you take me with you?" I'd ask, hoping they'd change their minds.

Mom's eyes would flash with righteous indignation. "And have you miss school? Not on your life, young man. Besides, you have your chores to do."

A few days later, Mom and Dad would pack up the Chevy sedan and drive off into the setting sun. I'd watch the trail of dust gradually disappear behind the car and prepare myself for the inevitable.

Wayne was a child molester. He first molested me when I was six years old, not long after he started working on our farm. Twice I told my mother about it, but she didn't believe me, dismissing the subject as unfit for discussion. I never talked to anyone else about it, and I don't think anyone would have believed me anyway. And if they had believed me, they would likely have tried to sidestep the issue, hoping (maybe praying) the problem would somehow just go away.

Unfortunately for me, it didn't go away. Wayne went after me whenever he could, whenever an opportunity presented itself. Even if my mom was gone for just a few hours, he'd come looking for me. With Mom and Dad gone for more than a week, there was no escaping Wayne.

Wayne would corner me near the family radio, where I'd be sitting listening to one of my favorite shows. He'd sneak up slowly, and eventually, I'd feel his long, bony fingers on my shoulder. As soon as he touched me, I wanted to scream, but I never did. I wanted to run away, but where would I go? Who could help me? Instead, my mind went numb.

No one in my family ever showed me any physical affection, not even my mother. I was aching to feel loved. But what Wayne did was wrong, so very wrong! I knew it, and certainly Wayne knew it, but that didn't prevent him from continuing to molest me.

If only Dad were here, I'd think. *If only he were sober. If only his hands could rest on my shoulders instead of Wayne's.* How I longed for a father's love! Instead, I found the nightmarish "gentleness" of Wayne Bailey.

Two weeks would pass before Mom and Dad returned home. As soon as she got in the door, Mom would ask, "Did you obey Wayne?" I would nod that I had. Mom would look at Wayne and he'd nod, always with that little smirk. Putting his hands on my shoulders, Wayne would tell my mom that I had been a good boy.

———

My Dad never said anything or asked any questions after returning from a trip. As soon as he got home, he was off looking for one of his wine bottles he'd left hidden around the farm. I'd found most of them while he was away and peed in all of them. I knew he'd never know the difference. And he'd be drunk soon enough.

Whenever we knew neighbors were coming to visit, I'd take matters into my own hands. First, I'd drive my Dad's pickup truck around the back of the barn and park it where no one coming onto the property would see it. I'd open the barn door wide and leave it open. Then I'd go and find Dad. I'd horse-collar him and drag him into the barn. I was getting pretty strong from working on the farm; my dad was short and thin. When he was full of booze, he didn't put up much of a struggle—even when he knew full well what I was about to do to him.

When Dad was full of booze, he didn't put up much of a struggle.

14

I'd drag my dad into the barn and hog-tie him to one of the stalls with one rope around his arms and a second rope around his neck and feet. I didn't believe in God, but I probably prayed that Dad would choke himself during the night in the barn. Because that's where he was going to stay until morning.

When company would arrive and ask for him, I'd say, "Oh, he had to leave for a while" or, "He had an appointment in town." They wouldn't ask any more questions; they'd just nod politely and walk into the house.

Later that night, I'd lie awake in bed wondering if maybe I should slip out to the barn and tighten the rope around my dad's neck a little more. Just enough to help him pass into eternity. But the police would probably figure out that I did it, and I'd be sent to jail or the reformatory. (I wasn't sure where they would put a thirteen-year-old who had killed his father, but surely they'd put him someplace he'd rather not be.)

═══════

I was reaching puberty now—my muscles were developing. I clenched my left fist and rapped my knuckles against the wall next to my bed. There was at least one very good use for my increased strength, and it was time to put it to the test the next time Mom and Dad were gone. I didn't have to wait long.

With my parents gone again, it seemed only a matter of minutes before I sensed Wayne standing behind me. I stiffened because I knew what was next. He did too. My fear and nervousness had never stopped Wayne before. As he drew closer I bit my lip. I wanted him to come a little farther. Just a little. His face was so close I could smell his foul breath.

I suppose his eyes were shut by then. That's what I was counting on. I spun around and slammed Wayne against the wall. Now it was my turn to breathe into his face. I got as close as I could without my body touching him, all the while squeezing him around the neck with my left hand. I raised my clenched right fist in front of him. "If you ever touch me again—even once—I'll kill you!"

One voice said to finish him off, and the other said to stop.

When Wayne didn't respond, I squeezed his neck tighter. It was as if I was hearing two voices simultaneously, one speaking in one ear and one in the other. One voice said to finish him off, and the other said to stop.

Wayne looked at me, desperately trying to take a breath. I was choking him so hard he couldn't talk. He moved his eyes up and down. I took it as a yes. I grudgingly released my grip, and he slid to the floor, holding his neck and coughing.

Wayne never touched me again. Several years later, he quit his job on the farm and left for good.

4

By the time I was a senior in high school, things were looking up for me. I was starting halfback on the football team and a standout guard on the basketball team. My grades were solid, and I began pocketing some extra cash repairing cars part-time.

I had a lot of friends at school too. I even found surrogate parents, thanks to my athletic prowess. They encouraged me, were there at all my games, and cheered me on, because my parents never came to any of my games—my father for obvious reasons, my mother because she was too heavy to get around or sit on the narrow bleachers.

A couple of months before graduation, I came home from a date one night and heard my mother crying. I ran through the house looking for her, while at the same time looking for my dad. *If he's done anything to her . . .* I didn't finish the thought; I just clenched my fists.

I found Mom in bed, crying. Sure enough, she had been beaten, but she defended my dad's behavior as usual. And I grew angry as usual. There was no defense for my dad's actions. There never had been and never could be. I'd find him and do to him what he had done to her.

As I turned to leave, Mom said, "Sit down, Son,," motioning to the side of the bed. Her eyes held me. So did her voice. There was something different about her voice, something unsettling. I sat next to her on the bed.

Twice before, Mom had left Dad, always promising to come back and get me. The first time, she went to Chicago and found a job working as a personal chauffeur for a couple too old to drive. The second time, she went off to Battle Creek. Both times, my father sobered up for a while and begged her to come home. And, eventually, she did. Then Dad would start to drink again, start to beat her again. The cycle would repeat itself, including my mom's excuses that he didn't really mean it, that he'd change. What a joke! My dad change? Yeah, sure . . . and elephants fly.

My brothers and sisters had all left the farm and never returned. Who could blame them? Now I was about to leave too. Maybe that was part of what was on Mom's mind as she looked at me and said, "I want to wait until you graduate from high school. Then . . . I want to die."

"Cut the joking, Mom," I said.

She turned her eyes from mine and looked across the room at the wall. We didn't have paintings or pictures hanging in the house; I wondered what she could be looking at so intently. "Your dad has broken my heart," she said.

"He's broken everybody's heart, Mom. He broke your heart years ago."

Mom nodded silently as the tears streamed down her face. "Yes. Yes he did. The difference now is . . . I can't take it anymore."

I started to speak, began to make promises to her, but she cut me off. "Promise me three things," she said.

I waited for her to continue. "Promise me three things," she whispered.

I nodded.

"Promise me you'll never be an alcoholic."

I nodded again.

"That you won't swear."

I wasn't sure how I'd keep that one, but I promised her.

"Promise me you'll bo the type of son I can be proud of."

"And that you'll be the type of son I can be proud of."

I lost it on that one. In spite of myself, I started to cry. *This is not happening,* I reasoned. *She couldn't die. Someone else might die, but not my mom.*

"Promise me," she said.

"I promise." I gripped her hand tightly, and she settled back on the bed. As she closed her eyes, I waited a few moments, then stood to leave. From the doorway, she looked peaceful, resting and breathing easier. *She'll be better by tomorrow,* I thought to myself. *So will Dad after he spends the night in the barn.* I walked silently from the room.

Graduation was uneventful. I got my degree and a few weeks later joined the Air National Guard with several of my high school buddies. We were at an age when the allure of danger that went with active duty seemed exciting. But in true military fashion, when training orders arrived, my friends were dispatched to Lackland Air Force Base near San Antonio, Texas, without me. That wouldn't do. We were a band of warriors, and we needed to stick together! I went to see the recruiter, an air force captain.

"I want to be with my friends," I told him.

"Can't be done," replied the captain, sorting through a thick stack of papers.

"Don't say can't to me, sir." The captain looked up at me sharply. I added, "With respect, sir, I don't believe in the word *can't*."

He looked at me and smiled, measuring me up. "Well, there is one way," he remarked.

"Yes, sir?"

"You can enlist in the regular air force and join them at Lackland."

"I can?"

"Yes, you can."

"I can enlist," I nodded.

"You can enlist."

"In the regular air force?"

"The regular air force."

I rolled my tongue around in my cheek and tried to

imagine what four years in the air force would be like. The captain returned to his stack of papers. "I'll do it," I said. A few moments later, I was reciting the oath of enlistment. Even as I spoke the words, other words reverberated inside my head: *This is not a good idea*.

As it turned out, my stint in the air force wasn't the ordeal I had imagined. First, I met my short-term goal of being with my buddies for two weeks (a ridiculous reason for joining the military, I'll admit), and once I was in the service, I decided to make the most of it. I had always enjoyed working on mechanical things and was assigned to work on the repair and maintenance of C-124 cargo aircraft at the base in Dover, Delaware. However, the powers that be concluded there was an even better use of my time than working on aircraft. My athletic abilities landed me a spot on the base's basketball team, and I traveled up and down the eastern seaboard, including to Bermuda, competing with teams from other air force bases. It was an honor that reflected well on the unit, and in return, my platoon leader cut me a lot of slack.

A heavy exhaust pipe caught me squarely across the head; everything went black.

I did have to pull duty sometimes. One day, while walking past a scaffold in the hangar where two men were working on a C-124, I heard someone shout a warning above me. I looked up in time to see what the men had dropped—a heavy exhaust pipe. There was no time to move out of the way. The pipe caught me squarely across the head; everything went black.

I woke up in a naval hospital in Philadelphia. A battery of tests revealed damage to the right side of my brain from cerebral swelling. The doctors kept me in the hospital for three months; it seemed like an eternity. Then one Friday afternoon—I remember that it was Friday the thirteenth—an air force chaplain came to my room.

Why is he standing in the doorway like that? I wondered. *Why doesn't he come inside the room?*

The chaplain kept turning his hat around in his hands. Finally he said, "Are you airman McDowell?"

"Yes, I am."

"I'm Chaplain Gardiner," he continued. I stiffened. No way was I going to let this man pray for me. I held his eyes in an icy stare. He looked away. *That's better,* I thought.

"I'm afraid I have to give you some bad news," said the chaplain.

Bad news, I scoffed. *Let the doctors tell me, not this guy.*

"It's your mother," said the chaplain.

"My mother?" I sat up in the bed.

"She died this morning."

5

The trip from Pennsylvania to Michigan seemed to take forever. I hitchhiked most of the way. A cold wind was blowing off Lake Erie, and snow began to fall about a hundred miles from home. I tried to keep myself warm with memories of the one person in my life who I believed loved me, even though she had not appeared to show much love when I was growing up. Instead, my thoughts were filled with our conversation two months before my high school graduation.

I want to see you graduate from high school, and then, I just want to die. . . .

Your dad has broken my heart. . . .

Promise me three things . . .

I want to see you graduate from high school, and then, I just want to die.

If it hadn't been my mother who had died, the doctors wouldn't have permitted me to leave the hospital. Because of my head injury, I was suffering from partial amnesia; I'd wake up at odd hours not knowing where I was or sometimes not knowing who I was.

Somehow, I got home. When I pushed the old screen door open and walked into the house, it was cold, so cold. No one had lit the stove. I walked around, wondering where everyone was. I poked my head inside my mother's bedroom. The covers on the bed were partially thrown back. It looked as if someone had just been sleeping there. Instinctively, I looked behind me, calling down the hallway, "Mom?" No answer.

I went to the other rooms. My brother's room . . . Wayne Bailey's former room upstairs.

I could hear the sound of a door to the house opening. I remained quiet. Footsteps creaked on the hallway floorboards. Whoever it was had entered my mother's room. I walked slowly downstairs.

I saw him sitting next to the bed, his back to the doorway. The wind outside was blowing harder now, and freezing rain pelted the windows. Then I saw my father pick up an edge of the sheet and wipe it across his face.

I looked at him for a moment, then walked outside. Dad had left the keys to his pickup in the ignition. I drove into town to find my mom's doctor and find out what had happened. He told me my mom had been in bed for several days when she died. "Internal hemorrhaging," he said.

"Did you see her face before she died?" I asked.

"Her face?"

"Did you notice the look in her eyes?"

The doctor looked at me quizzically, not sure what

I was driving at. "How would you describe the look in her eyes?" I continued.

"I don't know. When I got there, she had already passed."

"I see."

"There was nothing I could do, son," he said.

I nodded and stood to leave. The doctor had patients waiting. He shook my hand, telling me how sorry he was. *Say what you want,* I thought as I walked down the sidewalk toward my dad's pickup truck. *I know why my mother died.* I got inside the truck and sat behind the wheel. Freshly fallen snow had completely blanketed the windshield. I was enclosed in a strange, luminescent cocoon. I began grinding my teeth and gripped the steering wheel so hard that it seemed I would break it apart. "I know why my mom died," my reverie continued aloud. "My mom died of a broken heart. Say what you will . . . my mom died of a broken heart."

"I know why my mom died. . . . She died of a broken heart."

I looked out at the empty whiteness. I wanted to cry. I wanted to cry like I had that night beside my mother's bed. But I couldn't cry. I started up the engine and drove back to the farm.

The funeral was small, held at the grave site. *Mom is finally getting the peace she always wanted.* Soon I was hitchhiking back to the naval hospital in Pennsylvania.

6

A few months later I received a medical discharge from the air force and drifted back to the Midwest. I wasn't sure where to go, but one place I was determined to avoid was the farm. I ended up in Chicago, close to where my sister Shirley lived. I found a job repairing and doing routine maintenance on refrigeration units of eighteen-wheelers hauling meat and produce cross-country.

There were a few basic points to the job, all of which I was taught on my first day at work. A guy named Joe showed me the ropes. He pulled his car up next to a truck that had been left for servicing and began to siphon gasoline from the truck into large barrels. I looked around nervously. "Don't worry," Joe said with a grin. "The driver won't be back for four or five hours."

"I was thinking about the boss, not the truck driver."

Joe laughed. "The boss? Who do you think taught *me* the ropes?"

Joe proceeded with my orientation. He and another guy named Jerry unscrewed the bolts on the refrigeration unit, attached it to a winch, and pulled it out of the truck. Jerry then squeezed inside the trailer and began passing the bounty back to Joe and me. Hams, turkeys, boxes of steaks . . . it was a bonanza. Then the unit was serviced, put back in place, and the screws tightened as before. Presto.

When the unsuspecting driver returned for his truck, Joe and Jerry became accomplished actors with an impeccable sense of timing. They would usually be climbing off the rig, wiping their oily hands with shop rags, or walking around the semi with the concerned, solicitous look of hardworking men doing their part to keep America safe and prosperous. The driver would check the locks and seals on the doors of the trailer, sign the job ticket, and hit the road—usually fifty to a hundred pounds lighter than before. "Get over here, Josh," Joe would call to me.

"Give him a nice wave of the hand to send him on his way."

"Don't forget to smile," Jerry added. We stood in the garage doorway like the three amigos.

Was there an afterlife? I wondered. Was there a heaven and a hell?

I won't lie; I went along with it. But over time, my conscience began to get the better of me. I couldn't help remembering a promise I had made.

Be the kind of son I can be proud of.

Lying in my bed at night, I would sometimes turn my thoughts to where Mom might be. *Was there an afterlife?* I wondered. *Was there a heaven and a hell?*

Could there be a state of being where she continued to exist in some way, shape, or form? No one was there to answer my futile questions and I gradually fell asleep. Thankfully, I had worked hard enough during the day to drift off quickly.

━━━━━━━

Eventually, I quit my job and drove back to Michigan. I had saved more than enough money to call my own shots and enrolled at Kellogg College in Battle Creek for the fall term. My major was business, but my long-range plan was to go into law, and then politics. First, I'd become governor of Michigan, then a U.S. senator. After that, who knew? Maybe president of the United States. It all seemed clear to me. And attainable.

My English teacher and freshman counselor, Mrs. Hampton, gave me a reality check. "You have remarkable determination, Josh, more than I see in most students. It should take you far."

I smiled at her from the other side of her desk. "I dunno if you heard or not. I'm running for freshman class president."

"Is that so?" she said, adding, "I hope you do well."

I nodded confidently. "Oh, I will."

"I do have one area of concern, Josh," said Mrs. Hampton.

I sat up a little.

"Your English is atrocious. Perhaps your high school teachers were not as serious about this area as they

might otherwise have been. I realize farmers and factory workers aren't always expected to use textbook English."

"I did okay in English," I said, my defenses raised.

Mrs. Hampton ignored me. "You consistently use double negatives and incorrect grammar. Your pronunciation is also poor. I suspect that's because your spelling is so bad." I slumped a little.

"However, if you're willing to work hard and apply yourself, I'm willing to help you."

I was willing. I knew that if I was to rise to the top in law or politics or any other profession, my grammar needed to be top notch. "You'll tutor me?" I asked.

"I'm willing," she replied.

"So am I," I said.

I worked hard, and my grades improved. I won the student elections and checked off the boxes next to the first six months of my thirty-year plan. Things were going great.

7

As a rising star on campus, I made it my business to get to know as many of the students and teachers as possible. I figured this would be good training for the real thing one day, when I was governor of Michigan or a U.S. senator or, well . . . you know . . . the Big Guy. There were all kinds of social groups and organizations on campus, and I made it my business to have the pulse of each one. I created my own mental black book, where I noted everyone who could advance my agenda.

One day after lunch, I was sitting in the cafeteria with some of my friends when the Christian "clique" waltzed in—six students and two professors. Everyone knew who they were and what they represented. When I say they were Christians, I mean they were outspoken Christians. To me, almost all of us were "Christians" on campus, at least as far as I understood the term, but this group was different. They acted as if their faith made a difference in their lives. I smirked whenever I saw them.

Phony smiles, I thought to myself as they laughed and chattered good-naturedly. *What in the world are they hiding?* I wondered. Just looking at them riled me

up, and I resolved to do something about them. They were too few in number for me to worry about the political fallout my attitude might create.

When they made their way to the table adjoining ours, I sat up a bit straighter. One of the guys at my table was telling a dirty joke but got quiet when the Christians sat next to us. I asked him why he had stopped short of the punch line. Embarrassed, he made a gesture toward the Holy Rollers nearby.

These Christians acted as if their faith made a difference in their lives.

"What do they care?" I responded caustically. "They probably won't even get it." I noticed out of the corner of my eye that this got the attention of the cutest girl among them: Toni. I warmed to my subject. "I mean Christians have two brains, don't they? How do they ever manage with one brain always out looking for the other?"

My friends at the table laughed, and I launched into a little joke of my own, speaking loudly enough for everyone to hear.

"There was this man stumbling through the woods one day, when he comes upon a preacher baptizing people in the river. The preacher smells the alcohol on the man's breath, grabs him by the arm, and says, 'Brother, are you ready to find Jesus?' The drunk says, 'Sure thing,' so the preacher dunks him in the water a few seconds, pulls him up and says, 'You find Jesus?' The drunk spits out some water and shakes his head no. So the preacher dunks him under again and holds him down longer this time."

I got out of my chair, continuing with the joke while I made my way over to the Christians' table. There was an empty seat next to Toni, so I sat down next to her.

"Then the preacher pulls the drunk up and asks him, 'You find Jesus yet?' The drunk shakes his head, and the preacher, feeling a little exasperated by now, dunks him under the water again and holds him down for maybe thirty seconds. One of the deacons taps the preacher on the arm and says, 'You better bring 'im up 'fore he drowns.' The preacher kind of comes to himself, you know, and gets the shakes like this. . . ." I imitated my idea of a Holy Roller preacher having a spiritual spasm.

"Then he brings up the drunk, and practically shouting, says, 'You find Jesus, my brother?' The drunk looks at the preacher, spits some water out of his mouth, and says, 'Are you sure this is where he fell in?'"

I allowed myself a smug grin as people at the surrounding tables broke into appreciative laughter. Even a few people at Toni's table smiled. But not Toni. "You don't like my joke?" I asked her. She ignored me.

"Perhaps you have a better one," I continued. "Or maybe an entertaining story . . . like Jonah and the big fish?" I looked over at my compatriots at the other table. "Now, there's a whopper, boys. Talk about the one that got away! By God, that fish gets bigger every time they tell the story."

I looked back at Toni. She appeared oblivious to my needling. "Or maybe Noah and his steamliner? You know that story?"

Another voice broke in, a grown man's voice. It was Professor Blakeslee, a history teacher. "Welcome to our table, Mr. McDowell."

"Nice to be here," I replied sarcastically. I looked around at the others at the table. Everyone had a kind or at least curious expression, and I felt angry again without knowing why. "What is it about you Christians, anyway?" I asked.

"What do you mean?" asked the professor.

"I mean, it's like you're in another world."

"I'm not sure what you mean. We're very much in this world. The same world you live in."

> **"What is it about you Christians, anyway? It's like you're in another world."**

"You act like you belong somewhere else."

"Oh, well, thank you." Professor Blakeslee smiled. I heard others at the table murmuring in agreement.

"I didn't mean that as a compliment," I said, looking around at the group. "I mean, you're always smiling or being friendly, but it's like you think you're better than everyone else."

At last Toni spoke up. "That's not true."

"No?" I challenged her.

"Not at all. We're changed people, but that doesn't mean we think we're better than anyone."

I gave Toni a flirtatious look. "So, how've you changed? You seem to be the real thing to me."

Toni's eyes flashed indignantly. "The Bible says, 'If anyone is in Christ, he's a new creation.'"

Now it was my turn to be irritated. "Oh, c'mon!" I shouted. "Don't give me that garbage!" In the momentary silence that followed, I noticed my friends at the other table had all drifted away. I continued with my rant. "The Bible, church . . . that's just religion, and if there's one thing I can't stand in life, it's religion!"

Toni turned and looked me squarely in the eye.

"I didn't say religion, mister, I said Jesus Christ. And Jesus Christ *does* change lives. Even the lives of hardheaded, egotistical men like . . . like . . ."

"Gimme a break. How could a man who lived two thousand years ago change someone's life today?"

"Like me?" I smirked. I was getting her to lose her cool. "Jesus Christ," I continued, saying his name like an epithet. "Gimme a break. You don't know what you're talking about. And even if he did exist—which is by no means proven—how could a man who lived two thousand years ago change someone's life today?" I raised my eyebrows at Toni and allowed myself a little grin.

"Well," Toni said, with a little grin of her own, "I guess that's something you'll have to find out."

"Find out? What's there to find out? The startling absence of truth behind your la-la land Christian fables?"

Oliver, another member of the group, spoke up. "I have a suggestion." I turned and looked at him. He was a short fellow with thick glasses and hair standing up on his head like straw. *Here's a goofball*, I thought.

"Disprove Jesus' resurrection," Oliver said, "and you'll disprove the claims of Christianity."

"Disprove the Resurrection?"

"Yes. Prove that Jesus Christ did not rise bodily from the dead, and the entire foundation on which Christianity is built will come tumbling down. It's just a suggestion. I mean, rather than try and discredit all of Christianity, you can take a shortcut by disproving this one cornerstone of the faith. Save yourself a lot of trouble."

"Prove that Jesus Christ did not rise bodily from the dead, and the entire foundation on which Christianity is built will come tumbling down."

"Now, there's an idea," I nodded.

"I'm quite serious about it," said Oliver. "Should be quite an eye-opener for you."

I put my hands on the table and looked around at the Holy Rollers. "Well, I'm serious too." I got to my feet.

"We'll look forward to seeing you again," the professor said kindly.

I looked at the professor and the others, feeling a tinge of embarrassment for my belligerence. If I couldn't keep my temper under wraps, they'd win the argument for sure. "The name's Josh."

The professor reached for my hand. "I've heard about you, Josh, but it's nice to meet you in person. I'm Francis Blakeslee."

"How do you do?" I said, shaking his hand.

Toni spoke up. "Next time you drop by for a visit, try and be better prepared."

"Prepared?" I replied caustically. This girl was feisty. I liked that. "Oh, I'll be prepared all right. I just hope you're prepared to judge the facts impartially and abandon your illusions in the face of the evidence."

"And you, Josh?" asked the professor. I turned to look at him. "Would the same be true for you?"

I laughed hard. "I have no illusions, professor. I'm a realist."

"Just checking."

These are strange folk, I thought to myself, walking off. I pictured their faces when I presented my case for the myth of the Resurrection. *Would they be smiling then?* I imagined their befuddled and helpless looks. There was just one problem. I needed to assemble a case.

The college library wasn't much help. After a few hours, I realized I would need a great many more resources than they had available. And funny how these things happen—well, being young and impetuous certainly offers a partial explanation—but an idea popped into my head. I would go to Europe to study the original documents and manuscripts housed in the old libraries there.

For the remainder of the term, I focused on my studies and leadership responsibilities and saved up my money, and in May 1959 I took a Boeing 707 across the Atlantic to England.

8

My first stops were Oxford and Cambridge, followed by several libraries in London. Everywhere I went, I searched for the writings of skeptics—people who distrusted the claims of the Christian faith intellectually. I was confident that an independent analysis of the trial, crucifixion, and so-called resurrection of Jesus would prove that the story was simply a myth.

At the same time, I realized any lawyer worth his salt needed to understand how the defense would present its case. So I also studied the writings of skeptics who *became* Christians in spite of their skepticism—there were a few of them. Professional, educated men and scholars like C. S. Lewis and Frank Morison, a lawyer who wrote a book entitled *Who Moved the Stone?* Morison's conclusion in his book was disturbing. "There may be, and, as the writer thinks, there certainly is, a deep and profoundly historical basis for that much disputed sentence in the Apostles' Creed—*The third day he rose again from the dead.*"

There were other individuals who elicited my grudging respect, men like Lord Lyttleton and Gilbert

West. Both of these Oxford professors were convinced that Christianity was a "tale gone mad" and decided to work together to discredit it completely. Lyttleton set out to prove that Saul of Tarsus never converted to Christianity, while West sought to prove the fallacy of Christ's resurrection. When they came together later to compare their findings, they were shocked to discover that each had come to the opposite conclusion! In short order, they both became ardent followers of Jesus Christ. Lord Lyttleton would write, "The conversion and apostleship of Saint Paul alone, duly considered, was of itself a demonstration sufficient to prove Christianity to be a Divine Revelation."

Then there was the case of Professor Thomas Arnold. He was the former chair of history at Oxford, and author of the multivolume classic *History of Rome*. Well-educated in the study of historical facts, Arnold stated, "I have been used for many years to study the histories of other times, and to examine and weigh the evidence of those who have written about them, and I know of no one fact in the history of mankind which is proved by better and fuller evidence of every sort, than the great sign which God has given us that Christ died and rose again from the dead."

But I wouldn't be convinced so easily. After all, equally great intellects had come to opposite conclusions. I packed my knapsack and set out for continental Europe, traveling through France, Germany, and Switzerland. Over the next five weeks I visited the famous museums and libraries of Paris, Heidelberg,

Mainz, Geneva, and Zurich. Even though I didn't speak a word of French or German, much less Greek or Hebrew, I was enamored with the idea of setting my eyes on the actual manuscripts passed down through the centuries and touted as the original documentation, or close copies, of the original texts.

Finally, I made my way back to London, knowing I'd be returning home in a few days. I caught a bus to a small library that had escaped my attention before, located on the northeastern side of town. The librarian helped me locate the books I wanted, and I sat down to continue my research at about two thirty in the afternoon.

Four hours later, I leaned back in my chair, rubbed my eyes, and stared up at the ceiling. The words escaped my mouth before I could pull them back: "It's true." I had read the sources, had looked at every piece of evidence I could find, and they all pointed to one conclusion.

I had read the sources, had looked at every piece of evidence I could find, and they all pointed to one conclusion.

I repeated the words. "It's true." And a third time. "It really is true." This was one time too many for the librarian. She gave me a withering look that made me turn my eyes back to the book in front of me. But I couldn't see the book or read the words on the page. I could only think of where this truth might now lead.

I walked out of the library in the dusk of a London summer's day and headed down the sidewalk lost in thought. My research had brought me to the conclusion that the Bible of today is, in fact, an accurate text reporting actual events. This wasn't the conclusion I had expected to arrive at or desired to find; my goal had been to refute Christianity and Jesus' resurrection. But the historical evidence all pointed the other way. I realized my rejection of the Bible and Christianity had been based more on emotion than intellect.

On the long trip back to Michigan, I had a lot to think about.

Back at school, as I kept going over and over my discovery about the truth of the New Testament, I found it hard to sleep at night. My grades began to suffer; I couldn't get this newfound truth out of my mind. At the end of December I went to the church I had visited a few times with Toni, the only place she would go with me on a date.

9

I was sitting in Factoryville Bible Church with a friend, Larry Minor. The pastor, Fay Logan (*What a funny name*, I thought), was preaching. He had met me previously and knew about my "search for the truth." In fact, the times that I had come to a service with Toni, I had often challenged Pastor Logan on points in his sermons. I can't say that he prepared a special sermon for me that evening, but toward the end, it certainly seemed like it.

"Let's be clear," Pastor Logan said, drawing to a close. "God's salvation is not an intellectual exercise. In fact, the Bible says God has chosen the foolish things of the world to confound the wise." It seemed the pastor looked directly at me when he added, "So how then are we saved?" He turned the pages in his Bible and read from the tenth chapter of the book of Romans, written by the apostle Paul: "If you confess with your mouth the Lord Jesus and believe in your heart that God has raised him from the dead, you shall be saved. For with the heart man believes unto righteousness, and with the mouth confession is made unto salvation."

Beads of sweat began building on my forehead like

miniature storm clouds. Then the pastor continued. "So where are you today? Have you confessed with your mouth that Jesus is Lord? Do you believe in his resurrection? And if you do believe, are you ready to commit? Let's review what that commitment will entail. . . ."

Pastor Logan reviewed the main points of coming to faith in Jesus Christ: acknowledging one's sins, believing that God raised Jesus from the dead, and confessing Jesus as Lord and Savior. Then he invited anyone who wished to receive Christ to come forward.

I remained glued to my seat. To put it simply, I was afraid. Something inside seemed to prompt me to go forward, but at the same time, I was afraid of what my friends would say. They would think I was committing intellectual suicide. Pastor Logan repeated his invitation and waited to see who would respond. I wanted to disappear. Only a few months before, I had lambasted Christianity as a crutch for weak-minded fools. And then, setting out to expose its errors and contradictions, I had been intercepted by evidence to the contrary. Greater minds than mine had reached the unmistakable conclusion that Christ had risen from the dead.

But it wasn't the evidence for Christ's resurrection that made me break into a cold sweat that autumn evening in Factoryville, Michigan. It was something else. Something that even today makes me weep when I think about it. It was God's love. His unmistakable, obsessive love for me, a sinner! That truth alone made my head swim. I remember thinking, *God became a man named Jesus, and he is passionate about having a relationship with me.* With me! But how . . . how could God love me? Why would he love me?

When I was eleven years old, I had cursed and sworn I would hate God the rest of my life. Now I was overwhelmed by his love and acceptance. It broke me. The pastor repeated his invitation again, quoting Jeremiah 31:3: "I have loved you with an everlasting love; therefore with lovingkindness I have drawn you."

"Want me to go up with you?" Larry asked me. His question was just the motivation I needed. I was out of my seat in a flash and down at the altar.

Most everyone in church was surprised, I think. They knew how cynical and antagonistic to Christianity I had been. I'll never forget the look in Pastor Logan's eyes as I stood at the altar in front of him. I felt like a wayward son coming home. We said a prayer together, and afterward Pastor Logan took me aside to better explain what it meant to be a Christian. He must have spent about an hour with me; it marked the beginning of a long and rewarding discipleship under this wise and devout man.

> *God became a man named Jesus, and he is passionate about having a relationship with me. But why would he love me?*

When I left the church later that evening with Larry, I stopped in the parking lot to breathe in the cool night air. I felt like a man who had been lost in the desert and had found an oasis. I didn't know what to say or who to thank. I just wanted to drink the water. I looked up at the moon and smiled, even as warm, salty tears rolled down my face to the edges of my mouth. I asked God again to forgive me for the hardness of my heart, and again, mysteriously and tangibly, I felt his presence, his warmth and acceptance. I grasped the fact that my life would be forever changed. I wanted that moment to last forever.

I felt like a man who had been lost in the desert and had found an oasis.

10

Winter was long and cold that year, but the fire of a new life in Christ burned steadily within me. I continued my studies at Kellogg College, and Pastor Logan continued mentoring me in the basics of the Christian faith. Inevitably, the subject of forgiveness arose, and I knew I had a job to do.

A few months later, I was heading to downtown Battle Creek to meet my dad at a diner. Approaching the restaurant, I saw him sitting at a table next to the window, drinking coffee. He spotted me first, I think, because he looked quickly away when I caught sight of him. Even though I had called the meeting, I now wished I hadn't.

I entered the diner and sat across the table from Dad and his new girlfriend. "This is my son, Josh," he said to her. She nodded fearfully, extending her hand slowly toward mine. I could only imagine what Dad must have said to her about me.

"What can I get for you, hon?" asked the waitress, appearing from nowhere.

"A cup of coffee, please," I replied.

My dad gestured with his hand. "Get somethin' to eat. My treat."

I shook my head. Coffee would be fine. For the next several moments Dad and I glanced uncomfortably at one another off and on. Small talk did nothing to bridge the gap that seemed to stretch endlessly between us. I was becoming impatient. *I'll just tell him how it is and let him take it or leave it.* "Dad . . ." I began.

Anticipating a bombshell, my dad tensed his wiry body like a dog who knows he's about to be kicked. "Dad," I repeated, struggling to get the words out. And then, finally, "Dad, I love you."

I don't know who was more surprised—him hearing what I said or me saying the words. I absolutely did not want to love my father or forgive him. I was convinced he was responsible for my mother's death and for destroying our family. For years, I had gone to bed at night dreaming up ways to kill him without getting caught. Here I was, a new Christian, still determined to hate him. But something greater than hatred had seized control of my heart.

I absolutely did not want to love my father or forgive him.

The silence was awkward. I looked into my coffee cup as if it held tea leaves revealing the future. Finally, my father's querulous voice broke the impasse. "How can you love a father like me?" he asked.

I didn't want to answer him. Not then, anyway. But Pastor Logan had taught me too well. "I'm a Christian now," I said simply. I looked away and so did he. I don't know what he was think-ing. Even then, I breathed a silent prayer that God would allow me to keep hating this man who had destroyed his own family. But it wouldn't stick. The hatred continued to slip away. I quickly formed words in my mind to tell him about all the harm he had caused to the ones he was called to love and protect. But I knew that if I opened my mouth, the same words would emerge as before: "I love you."

That's when I knew Christianity was real.

Not knowing what else to do or say, I left the diner without saying another word.

> **I prayed that God would allow me to keep hating this man who had destroyed his own family. But the hatred continued to slip away.**

11

Pastor Logan was pleased to hear how the meeting with my father had gone. Thinking back on the awkward conversation, I wasn't as convinced. "Obedience to God's commands," he said, "is not an emotion but an action."

"We're called to obey," I added. "The outcome is in God's hands."

"Exactly," the pastor said, smiling. "Which brings us, I feel, to someone else who has figured prominently in your life."

Instantly, I knew who he was talking about and regretted having said anything about obeying God. I could almost perceive my childhood tormentor's rancid breath hanging in the air. I got out of my seat and began pacing the floor in Pastor Logan's study. "No way," I said, finally. "You can't be serious."

"I'm perfectly serious, Josh."

"It's impossible, Pastor."

"All things are possible with God."

I looked at Pastor Logan as if he were stabbing me in the back. "I told you all about him, pastor. You know what he did to me for years; besides, who knows how many other boys and young men were his victims after me? How can you ask me to forgive him? I hope he burns in hell! I'll escort him there myself!"

Pastor Logan looked into the fire that burned steadily in the fireplace. "Your forgiveness does not justify or condone what he did, Josh. But it does set in motion the process whereby you free yourself of the chains of the past. It allows you to move on in life and also provides a lost soul with the opportunity for redemption."

"How can you ask me to forgive Wayne? I hope he burns in hell!"

Now it was my turn to stare into the fire. "If this is what Christianity requires, Pastor, maybe I should just hang it up. I understand that in an ideal world forgiveness is the right thing to do. But you're asking too much of me. I cannot forgive Wayne Bailey."

"I'm not asking you to forgive Wayne Bailey, Josh."

"But God is," I added. It was more a question— a defiant one at that.

Pastor Logan was silent a moment. I looked over at him. He was a good man but powerless to alter the fundamental course of my life. It was too late for that. The wood crackled in the fire, and I spoke to myself as much as to him when I said, "No one understands. No one."

Pastor Logan looked at me as if he wanted to say something. Instead, he reached for his Bible. He cleared his throat and began to read from the New Testament: "And when they had come to the place called Calvary, there they crucified Him, and the criminals, one on the right hand and the other on the left. Then Jesus said, 'Father, forgive them, for they do not know what they do.'"

I interrupted his reading. "Wayne Bailey knew exactly what he was doing."

"So did Jesus," replied Pastor Logan.

━━━━━━

Initially I remember hoping that I wouldn't be able to find out where Wayne lived. But I did find out and called him on the phone. The conversation was brief. I told him I was coming to see him.

He lived in a drab apartment in Jackson, Michigan. When I knocked and he opened the door, I immediately noticed that he didn't keep his own place as nice as he had kept his room in our house. There were no teacups or parakeets in the apartment—just a graying, worn-looking man with troubled eyes. I got right to the point.

"Wayne, what you did to me was evil. Very evil! But I've come to know Jesus Christ as Savior and Lord. And I've come here . . . to . . . tell you . . ." My carefully rehearsed words failed me. I prayed for strength and realized that what I had to say didn't need a script. I sighed deeply.

"Wayne, all of us have sinned, and no one measures up to God's standard of perfection. We all need redemption, and, well, I've come here to tell you something you need to hear."

He looked at me, his pale blue eyes unblinking. For a moment, I wished it wasn't true, but it was true and I had to say it. "Christ died for you, Wayne, as much as he did for me."

After a few moments I walked to the door, turning to face him a final time. "One other thing, Wayne. Don't let me ever hear of you touching a young man again. You'll regret it."

I walked out to the parking lot and got into my car. *Where is the emotion?* I asked myself, starting up the engine. *Where is the euphoria I should feel after staring down the demons of my past?* I pulled out of the parking lot and made my way to the highway. And then it hit me. There was peace in my heart. A peace unlike anything I had experienced before. I had chosen to forgive an enemy out of obedience to God's command, and I had the steady, full peace the Bible describes as surpassing human understanding.

It rained most of the way during the one-hour drive back to Battle Creek.

━━━━━

When I walked into Pastor Logan's study for my next midweek discipleship class, he greeted me with "I've been thinking, Josh."

"Is that so? I thought you were always thinking," I replied.

Pastor Logan smiled and stood up behind his desk. "Why don't we take a walk? It's a beautiful day."

It was late spring, and the Michigan countryside was thick with the green of trees and an artist's palette of color from wildflowers. "I like how Martin Luther put it," said Pastor Logan, as we walked down a path through the woods behind his house. "He said 'God writes the gospel not just in the Bible, but also on trees, in the flowers, and on the clouds and stars.'" I nodded. I knew this was not what Pastor Logan had been thinking about nor what he wanted to talk about, but I held my peace. "Have you ever heard of Wheaton College?" he continued.

"No," I replied. "Where's that?"

"Outside Chicago. It's where Billy Graham went to school."

"Billy Graham?"

"Yes, Billy Graham. It's a top-notch Christian liberal arts college. I think you should transfer there for your junior and senior years."

"Why?"

"You're ready for the next steps, Josh. I've taken you about as far as I can."

I stopped walking so he would turn and look at me. "Pastor Logan, it's difficult to imagine any college or college professor taking the time and interest in me that you have."

"Be that as it may, Josh, my knowledge and education only extend so far." He continued walking, and I fell into step alongside him. "Wheaton is no cakewalk. It will demand a great deal from you academically, but . . ." He turned to look at me with that soft, encouraging smile of his. "I think you're up to the challenge."

"Will it help prepare me for the legal profession?"

"Whatever you decide to do, Wheaton will help you excel. They don't ordinarily take transfer students, but I know some people there, and I'll recommend you highly. If you like, I can make some calls, and we'll see what happens."

"Yes sir, I think that would be great." We continued walking. I breathed in the sweet fragrance of the day, admiring God's gospel in the trees and flowers around me, the billowing clouds, and the blue Michigan sky.

12

I entered Wheaton College as a junior in the fall of 1960. At first, I felt like a man who didn't know how to swim and had been pushed headfirst out of a boat into a lake. I only had time for two things—studying and working. The academic side was by far the more demanding of the two, but I also juggled a part-time job in the afternoons delivering paper and important documents to area high schools.

The town of Wheaton, Illinois, is bisected by the railroad tracks that connect the suburbs to Chicago. One afternoon, I was waiting in my car at a railroad crossing when a train began to pass. It was a warm day for that time of the year, and I began to doze off. Suddenly I opened my eyes and saw a pickup truck approaching in my rearview mirror. I blinked and shook my head to make sure I wasn't asleep. The truck was barreling toward my car at breakneck speed—well over fifty miles per hour—and showed no signs of stopping. With the train in front of me, there was nowhere to go and scarcely time to react. The truck plowed into my Ford Falcon and sent my vehicle spinning like a top, breaking the crossing gate and propelling my car to within a foot of the train roaring past. A few inches more, and I would have been killed.

Still, the impact was so severe that I tore ligaments in my neck and down my back. After four days in intensive care, I spent another week and a half in the hospital. It was a lonely time. My dad never came to visit me. The doctors knew my recovery would be slow, so they sent me home to mend. Ironically, the man who had hit me was a drunk driver.

I rode to Union City, Michigan, strapped in a gurney in the back of an ambulance. It seemed to take forever. The paramedic

A truck was barreling toward my car at breakneck speed.

in the back with me wasn't talkative, and I couldn't turn my head to the right or left. Home was the last place in the world I wanted to be.

═══════

My dad was there to meet the ambulance when we arrived at the farmstead. I had been told that a nurse would be there, but she was late that day. To add to my surprise, Dad was sober.

He followed the attendants as they wheeled me to my room and lifted me from the gurney to my bed. They strapped me bodily to the bed, making sure my head could not move from side to side. After giving some instructions to my dad, the paramedics left the house. Over the next few minutes, I could hear two things—the sound of the ambulance driving away and a fly buzzing near my head. Then I heard some footsteps in the hallway outside my room.

From the corner of my eye, I could just make out the figure of my dad in the doorway. He stood there awhile, and as I strained my eyes to see him better, I noticed he was crying. Then he began to pace back and forth, not saying anything. I followed him with my eyes as best I could, but the effort made me tired. Moments passed; I don't know how long. And then I felt someone next to me.

Dad's tears began to fall on my face. "How can you ever love a father like me?"

I opened my eyes and saw my dad standing above me. He was still crying, and his tears began to fall on my face. His voice was hoarse, his words faltering. "How . . . can you ever . . . love . . . a father . . . like me?" I was speechless. Dad didn't wait for a response. He continued to pace again. A minute or so later, he was back at my side. "The diner," he said.

"The diner?"

"The diner in Battle Creek."

"Yes . . ."

"You said something to me. You said you loved me."

Now it was my turn to get emotional. "Yes, Dad, it's true." I hesitated for a moment. "I don't need to tell you

I've hated and despised you. But I don't feel that way anymore. I've learned one thing, Dad, and it's made all the difference in my life: God became man, and his name is Jesus. And Jesus is passionate about having a relationship with you."

> **"If Jesus can do in my life what I've seen him do in yours, then I want to know him."**

Dad was silent, and he disappeared from my line of sight. After a few moments, I could hear him walking out of the room. I'm not sure how much time passed. It was warm, and the fly was still buzzing around. Perhaps forty-five minutes went by before Dad came back in. He sat down on the edge of my bed and leaned down, making it easier for me to see him. Fresh tears streaked his face. *How could he still be crying?* I wondered.

"Son," he said, "if Jesus can do in my life what I've seen him do in yours . . . then I want to know him."

I tried to sit up in bed, but realized I couldn't move. "You need to ask him into your life, Dad. You need to open your heart to him and pray."

"I don't reckon I know how to pray, Son."

"Just tell him what's in your heart."

Dad nodded and made a simple, down-to-earth farmer's prayer. "God, if you are God," he said, "and if Christ is your Son . . . and if you can forgive me for what I've done to my family . . ." He paused for a moment, sighing deeply, then continued. "And if you can do in my life what I've seen you do in my son's life, then I want to place my trust in you as my personal Savior and Lord."

As my dad prayed, my eyes filled with tears, and his form became blurry to me, even though I continued to hear him clearly. The tears ran down my face, and I couldn't move my hand to wipe them away. It was as if I was looking up at my father from the bottom of a swimming pool. And then, after he had prayed, came the sweetest gesture of all. My dad wiped the tears from my eyes.

13

When I gave my life to Christ, I began to change over a period of a year. When my father came to Christ, the change was immediate. It was as if someone reached down inside him and turned on a light that immediately lit up a dark room. After that, he touched alcohol only once. He got it as far as his lips but no further.

As a result of my dad's decision to trust Christ, scores of people in that small town and the surrounding area also came to know Jesus Christ as Savior and Lord—all because of the town drunk whose life had changed. Dad also became active with Alcoholics Anonymous and visited prisons throughout the state, sharing the gospel and the story of his changed life with prisoners. If only my mother had lived to see that day.

Fourteen months later Dad died. Most of his stomach had been removed, and his liver had been destroyed by thirty years of heavy drinking.

I felt more alone than ever. At the same time, my life had taken on added purpose and direction. I graduated from Wheaton College and later attended Talbot Theological Seminary in California. I began to feel the call to be a speaker—to share, as well as defend, the Christian faith. In many ways I felt inadequate to the task, but I also realized that "if anyone is in Christ, he is a new creation; old things have passed away; behold, all things have become new." An early association with Campus Crusade for Christ (an on-campus Christian ministry geared to college-age students), one that still continues today, provided the organizational structure I needed and allowed me to be part of a team.

In June 1976 I sat down to write out my reasons for believing in Jesus, the Bible, and Jesus' resurrection— all the facts that had convinced me when I was a college student. I wrote nearly nonstop for forty-eight hours before I put my pen down. Nine months later, I held the first copies of my book *More Than a Carpenter*.

And so the years have passed. To date, I have traveled to 118 countries where I have been able to share the gospel with approximately 10 million young people. I have written or coauthored 115 books and given more than twenty-four thousand talks on more than a thousand university campuses.

On the personal front, God has allowed me to marry my phenomenal wife, Dottie, and with her raise four wonderful children. I now count the blessing of living to see my children's children, and—by God's grace— I continue to minister actively around the world.

My successes, however, such as they are, will never

take the place of my failures. It was my failures, you see, that provided the greatest impetus to my work and life.

When I came to Christ at the age of twenty, I was an insecure young man. I would hear constantly in church that God wanted us to offer our gifts and abilities in service to him. This created a problem for me, because I felt I had nothing to offer God. I was an emotional wreck from the scars of my childhood. I had a terrible temper. I struggled with grammar. I even had an embarrassing stutter that surfaced when I was stressed.

When I came to Christ, I felt I had nothing to offer God.

Then one day I prayed for God to take my brokenness and use it for his glory; I prayed for him to take the weaknesses of my life and use them for his strength. And that is just what he has done. He has taken the weak, damaged goods that have made up the life of Josh McDowell and converted them into a force—I trust—for his praise and honor. The glory is his and can only be his because apart from him, I am nothing.

And you, my friend? Perhaps you've had a stable upbringing. Or perhaps, like me, your life has been painfully dysfunctional. Maybe you're consumed with intellectual doubt as I was. Wherever you're coming from in life, there is but one way to God, our loving Father, and that is through his Son, Jesus Christ. Jesus said in John 14:6, "I am the way, the truth, and the life. No one comes to the Father except through Me."

Jesus is the doorway to eternal life. There is a wide,

easy road that most of us take here on earth. There is also a narrow road, defined by the person of Jesus Christ, that leads to eternal life. I promise you with all the love and conviction in my heart that God's invitation is extended to you—whoever you are, whatever you've done, wherever you're coming from—to join him on this narrow road. As Jesus says in Revelation 3:20, "Here I am! I stand at the door and knock. If anyone hears my voice and opens the door, I will come in and eat with him, and he with me" (NIV). Perhaps you will pray as my father prayed those many years ago when he said, "Jesus, if you can do in my life what I've seen you do in my son's life, then I want to place my trust in you as my personal Savior and Lord."

God has taken the weak, damaged goods of my life and converted them into a force for his praise and glory.

Will you pray this prayer with me? Will you surrender your will to the lordship of Jesus Christ? Truly he is passionate about having a relationship with you.

Father in heaven, I know I'm a sinner, and I know my sin separates me from you. But I believe you love me, and I believe that Jesus died for me on the cross at Calvary. I open my heart to you. I repent of my sins and ask Jesus to come into my heart and be my Lord and Savior. In Christ's name I pray. Amen.

Visit www.josh.org for articles, discussion guides, videos, devotionals, and other resources to learn more about God's love.